Be Still

21 DAYS OF DAILY INSPIRATIONS ON TRUSTING GOD TO LEAD YOU TO A PATH OF PEACE

By Tam Yvonne

Be Still – 21 Days of Daily Inspirations on Trusting God to Lead You to a Path of Peace © 2021 By Tam Yvonne

ALL RIGHTS RESERVED. No part of this book may be reproduced in any written, electronic, recording, or photocopying without written permission of the publisher or author. The exception would be in the case of brief quotations embodied in the critical articles or reviews and pages where permission is specifically granted by the publisher or author.

LEGAL DISCLAIMER: Although the author and publisher have made every effort to ensure that the information in this book was correct at press time, the author and publisher do not assume and hereby disclaim any liability to any party for any loss, damage, or disruption caused by errors or omissions, whether such errors or omissions result from negligence, accident, or any other cause.

Cover By: Christian Cuan
Edited By: Candice "Ordered Steps" Johnson
Publishing Services By: Charron Monaye
Formatting By: U Can Mark My Word, Carla M. Dean

Library of Congress Cataloging–in–Publication Data has been applied for.

ISBN: 978-1-7362575-0-00
PRINTED IN THE UNITED STATES OF AMER

Table of Contents

Dear Reader
Preface
Acknowledgements
Dedication
Day 1 – Awaken & Shine Like a Diamond
Day 2 – Unexpected Things
Day 3 – Accountability
Day 4 – Prayer Works
Day 5 – Patience
Day 6 – Anointed One
Day 7 – Self Love is Your Best Friend
Day 8 – Acceptance
Day 9 – Delayed, Never Denied
Day 10 – Forgiveness
Day 11 – Stand for Something or Fall for Anything
Day 12 – Stay Ready So You Don't Have to Get Ready
Day 13 – Lord, Lead Me
Day 14 – Finance is King
Day 15 – Life Lessons, the Best Teacher
Day 16 – Strength
Day 17 – What is the message of Job?
Day 18 – Keep Pressing On
Day 19 – What Are You Focused On?
Day 20 – Where Is My Boaz?
Day 21 – The Peace of God
BONUS DAY - Be Still
Epilogue
Prayer
Reflection Notes
About the Author

Be Still

21 DAYS OF DAILY INSPIRATIONS ON TRUSTING GOD TO LEAD YOU TO A PATH OF PEACE

Dear Reader,

Are you living a productive life, or are you busy being busy? Are you determined to get "it" done, or do you wait for God to send His approval? Are you moving to the beat of your own drum, or do you revel in the joy of patience? When was the last time you trusted God to lead you to a path of peace?

As an internationally acclaimed author, I have penned and published books detailing the importance of acknowledging, accepting, and attaining your position and purpose in life. As a woman of faith, I understand the importance of removing my hands from what God is already fixing on my behalf, as well as the power of obedience and discernment. With my eyes focused on God, I have learned to manifest the desires of my heart, simply by believing and walking in the steps He has ordered. I am who I am today, solely because I trusted God.

The Bible instructs us to "Trust in the Lord with all your heart and lean not on your own understanding; in all your ways submit to Him, and He will make your paths straight." (Proverbs 3: 5-6). The day I moved out of God's way was the day God relocated me, gave me financial freedom, helped me launch a prosperous business, and awarded me peace and love, beneficial for my goals.

Are *you* ready to do the work? Do you want to reach this kind of abundance?

In *Be Still: 21 Days of Daily Inspirations on Trusting God to Lead You to a Path of Peace,* best-selling author Tam Yvonne guides you through a step-by-step journey towards a deeper understanding of your desires through scripture, conversation and reflection. This devotional explores various topics about the most common situations we are faced with and must overcome, as Tam brilliantly illustrates the importance of owning your life, as well as providing readers with the keys and strategies to help them succeed.

I can tell you without reservation or question that when it comes to walking by faith and the word of God, Tam is the trusted advisor and virtuous woman in this subject matter. I know this because I've had the privilege of observing her extraordinary faith and winning strategies for myself.

Prepare to fully engage yourself in the advice given within these pages, and I look forward to hearing your testimony. Life is worth living, so trust God today.

Yours in Peace,

Charron Monaye

Founder of Pen Legacy, LLC.
Best-Selling, Award-Winning Author, Playwright & Speaker
www.charronmonaye.com

Preface

Why am I always dating the same type of person?
Why do I always end up in the same dead-end jobs?
Why is there so much evil and suffering in the world?
What does the future hold for me?

Do any of these questions sound familiar? Every day we ask so much of God, thank goodness He doesn't get tired of us. There are so many questions swirling through our minds throughout the day, that we tend to forget bringing those questions to God doesn't burden Him; in fact, casting our cares and concerns upon Him is what He has commissioned us to do. For instance, in our minds we may believe we've discovered the perfect mate. But have we taken the time ask God, "Is this the mate You have for me?"

TAM YVONNE

We work hard in college, only to graduate and accept a minimum wage paying job, when we expected way more return from our expensive degree. Or maybe we're weighed down by the evils of the world, wondering why people do some of the horrible things that they do? Spending energy on situations not in our power to change or control can be exhausting. Not to mention, trying to predict and direct our futures in the midst of it all is downright exhausting.

As humans, our instinct is to take control of our lives and pursue the things we want, but little do we know… that's where we mess up. Assuming the gargantuan task of controlling our own lives was never in God's plan for us; we must take our hands off the wheel and allow Him to steer us to our destination. It's time for us to allow God to do His job. He is way more equipped to handle our situations than we are; He doesn't want us to solve our own problems anyway. Don't you have enough to deal with in your life already? Why are you fighting for the Master's job, too? All God requires of us is to be patient, prayerful and keep the faith. **PPF: patient, prayerful, faith**! It's just that simple, y'all!

God promised in His word that He would never leave us nor forsake us. Believe that His will manifest in your life. By allowing God to pen your love story, bless you with that amazing job, guard your heart against evil and guide you to a future you never imagined, it will save you a lot of heartache, anxiety, disappointment and discouragement.

I created this 21-day devotional to encourage and give you hope when life brings you down. My goal? To be as transparent and real as I possibly can. I want to inspire you with my personal experiences as a divorced mother of two, suddenly thrust back into the dating world with no warning. My, that scene changed since I navigated my way through it during the late 90s! But that was just one facet of the woman I was back then.

I was a woman overworking myself at low paying job after low paying job, all the while trying to support myself and two minor children. Witnessing evil after evil, I couldn't fathom what God had for my future, because it became too hard to see. But I overcame it. Now I'm here to help you think, laugh, and to speak some truth! Beginning with loneliness. Don't you know God didn't create us to be alone? So for those of you seeking a true love of your own, God's Word specifically says so. If you don't believe me, go grab your Bible and turn to Genesis 2:18.

I'll wait…

See, I told you!

"Later, the Lord God said, 'It is not good for the man to be alone. I will make the woman to be an authority corresponding to him.'" Genesis 2:18 *(International Standard Version).*

The Lord makes His Word plain. I'm so excited to share my journey of following God's Word and how it opened my eyes and heart to be available for the man whom God has for me, the job He has for me and the future He's already laid out for my life.

I don't want to overwhelm you with fruitless words on a page, that's why my messages to you are short, sweet, straightforward and easy to follow. I want you to feel as if we're having a splendid conversation over a mug of green tea. This is more than small talk; I'm speaking encouragement over your life.

I pray that you'll read this devotional with an open heart and mind, and that by the time you finish, you won't have questions, but will have an open heart and mind to accept God's plans for your life. With that being said, I am excited to embark on this journey together! May the Lord continue to bless and guide your path to the peaceful life He has in store for you!

Always Be a Blessing,
Tam Yvonne

Acknowledgments

In everything I do and accomplish, all honor and praises go to the Great Almighty, the author of knowledge and wisdom, my Lord and Savior Jesus Christ, without whom none of this would be possible. I am so grateful for His love, mercy and grace!

My children - Sharon and Ellis are the best gifts I've ever received, and I'm so blessed to be their "Mommy."

Thank you to my sweetie-babe Rico, for your endless support, and your kind, loving and understanding spirit. To all of my relatives, friends, and others who have been consistent in my life and have shown your support, either spiritually, financially, morally or physically: I thank you.

My publishing team - Pen Legacy, LLC, the dedication that you all have shown me will forever be appreciated.

TAM YVONNE

Walter Cole, my marketing professional with Skyport Drones and D'Andria Jackson, my graphic designer with Debonair Designs, all I can say is that you two are amazing!

My personal heavenly angel - my grandma, who I know is always watching over me, and putting in a good word to the Lord on my behalf.

Finally, thank you to my readers, the Team Tam crew. Without you, I wouldn't be a best-selling author and wouldn't be here now, writing these words in my 2nd book. Every time you enthusiastically told friends and family members, "You have to read this book," it has put my books on the map towards greatness and I will be forever grateful! ♥

Dedication

This book is dedicated to all of God's daughters (my sisters in Christ), who have given their all to their families, spouses, children, jobs, churches, significant others…everyone but themselves. In the face of overwhelming circumstances and often being stretched too thin, you still manage to keep the faith that God truly has an amazing plan for your life. May our Lord and Savior Jesus Christ continue to bless you with His glorious love and protection.

*"Let go of what you think you want,
and allow GOD to do HIS job!
Amazing things happen when you BE STILL,
LET GO & LET GOD!"*
~Tam Yvonne~

Day 1
Awaken & Shine Like a Diamond~

Every day that we awaken is a reason to rise with celebration and thanksgiving, for no day is promised. It is up to you to set the tone for your day; why not rise with love in your heart, a smile on your face and a positive attitude to tackle whatever the day has in store for you? After all, you've been blessed to see another day's journey…why not wake up shining like a diamond?

This is the day that the Lord has made - rejoice and be glad in it!

"This is from the LORD—it is awesome in our sight."
(Psalm 118:23 ISV)

TAM YVONNE

Remember that each day that you arise with breath in your body is a gift from the Lord; your life is awesome in His sight.

What gift are you grateful for today?

_____
_____
_____
_____
_____
_____
_____
_____
_____
_____
_____
_____

Day 2

~ Unexpected Things ~

Always expect the unexpected.

Whether it's unforeseen heartbreak, a failure you were trying to avoid, sudden financial troubles, a surprise layoff or most recently - a pandemic without warning, the unexpected hits hard. Storms will arise in our lives, but please know trials don't last always; God is our shelter in time of storms. When trouble enters our lives, that's when you go strong in your prayer life. Take it to God, meditate on comforting scriptures, and surround yourself with people who are travel the same spiritual path as you. This is not the time to give up! Get up and face that circumstance head on, with the Lord leading the way. Allow your faith to guide you out of the darkness of the storm. Jesus is the way, the truth and the light in any circumstance.

"Jesus told him, 'I am the way, the truth, and the life. No one comes to the Father except through Me.'"

(John 14:6 ISV)

Daily Note

What storm(s) are you battling that you need to give to GOD?

_____

_____

_____

_____

_____

_____

_____

_____

_____

_____

Day 3

~ Accountability ~

Many of us don't truly understand what accountability is in our lives. Accountability is the personal relationship you have to grow closer to God. This relationship should provoke you to question, challenge, and encourage yourself to grow spiritually in the Lord. Your accountability to God should draw you closer to Him; as you grow closer, He will provide you with an accountability partner. God is faithful - all you have to do is ask Him to reveal who's for you, and to remove those who aren't. Don't give up hope.

"Consequently, each of us will give an account of himself to God."

(Romans 14:12 ISV)

Daily Note

How are you accountable to God?

Day 4
~Prayer Works~

Do you know that prayer works? That's a shout right there! Let me ask it one more time for those who didn't catch it the first time: Do you know that prayer works? I'm a living witness that when you go to God in prayer, He makes things happen. Now I'm not going to tell you answered prayers are immediate - you already know God works in His perfect timing, not ours. But my goodness, when God comes through, He comes through! Honey, when you take those storms and distractions we discussed on Day 2 to the LORD in prayer, it changes things. God changes things. I'm not saying the situation will be resolved the way we think it should be, but the breakthrough will come in such a such a way that you know it was nobody but God!

"You will receive whatever you ask for in prayer, if you believe."

(Matthew 21:22 ISV)

Daily Note

What have you asked GOD for in prayer? Has He delivered?

_____
_____
_____
_____
_____
_____
_____
_____
_____
_____

Day 5
~Patience~

I can write an entire book on patience. Now I've gotten better over the years, but being patient is something that I've never been very good at. If you live long enough to go through some things, life will teach you patience, whether you want it or not. When I was married, being a wife taught me patience. See, I learned that everyone wasn't brought up the same way that I was. Marriage was one thing, but stepping into motherhood was a whole different level of patience I had to conquer. Raising children is hard; it's even harder when you're the primary caregiver with no one to fall back on. You are the only plan for your children, and have to be patient enough to get past the growing pains. On the flip side, being a daughter taught me patience, too. So did my role as a sibling, friend, and most importantly a child of God. In every aspect of my life, I have learned to be patient, though at times it feels like I am waiting forever for God to fulfill His promises to me. *Where are my good things, Lord*? Even though I'm tempted to rush His miracles, God always delivers when He's ready for me to receive the blessings He has for me.

Sometimes, we think God doesn't hear our prayers and forgets His promises to us. But what I've learned in my over 40 years on this earth, is that God never forgets! All He requires of us is our obedience, to seek Him in prayer with thanksgiving and make our requests known before taking steps towards making those requests a reality. He'll do the rest. You must be faithful to God. You must be consistent with Him and have the will to take risks in life, knowing He has your back. Just be patient and let God lead you to your promises.

"I waited patiently for the Lord; and He inclined unto me, and heard my cry."

(Psalms 40:1 KJV)

Daily Note

What are you waiting patiently for?

Day 6
~Anointed One~

Take heed - Day 6 is a little lengthy.

Sitting here at the keyboard, typing about *the anointing*…I can feel my preacher hat coming on! Being anointed by God separates you from a lot of people, places and things. The blessings over your life set you apart. I don't know about y'all, but I knew at an early age that I was different and didn't quite fit in with the ways of the world. I rejoined the dating scene in my late 30's, after having been married for 12 years and got a huge reality check.

Whew chile, can you say: Don't fit in?

In the eight years I've been divorced, I have tried my hand at dating. I've dated older men, men my age, African American men, Latino men; white collar men, blue collar men, college educated men...and I still don't have a prince in sight.

The lack of male companionship in my life prompted me to thinking: Are my standards too high? So, I lowered them. Am I requiring too much? I stopped making my desires known. Maybe I'm too much for him. I watered down my awesomeness to make him feel good about himself. Time and time again, love didn't take a victory lap for me. So then I considered doing away with my boundaries. Ummm...NO. That's when I realized I had to draw the line. I will not accept anything less than what I want just to have a man in my life. Period.

I require a lot, because I give a lot; the right man will be able to handle all of me. My intelligence, my strength, my drive, my passion. My desires. I don't have to water myself down in order to make someone else feel worthy.

As a Woman of God, the man I want to pursue me will be secure and rooted in Christ. He's respectful, kind, handsome (inside and out), has strong character, he's stable and honest. Lastly, my ideal guy has a genuine relationship with the Lord that is rooted in truth.

TAM YVONNE

I used to feel some type of way about my inability to maintain a relationship longer than 2 ½ years after my marriage. When I noticed the women around me getting married after only months of dating, I got depressed and wallowed in pity parties. Was I less talented than they were? Less pretty? Not as smart? All these questions swirled through my mind and brought me down. Through my fog of negativity and clinging on to my potential mate checklist, the devil constantly sent men into my life whom I thought I desired…not realizing they were sent in disguise.

But just as He's done so often in my life, God proved not only me, but to others who might've looked down on me, whom He is and what He's done in my life.

The places He's taken His anointed one. The people that He has placed in His anointed one's life. The gifts and blessings He continuously bestows upon His anointed one. I could go on! See, God doesn't allow me to wallow in sadness or depression; He's got me too busy counting my blessings and flourishing in His perfect peace!

I know we all go through things and often feel like we're not enough. That we're "less than." We see others around us who don't work as hard or it seems things just fall into their lap, all the while you're working like crazy just to make things happen. Know that you are enough in the eyes of God, and that's all that really matters. You are anointed for a reason – HE CHOSE YOU!

"The Spirit of the Lord is upon me, because the Lord has anointed me; He has sent me to bring good news to the oppressed and to bind up the brokenhearted, to proclaim freedom for the captives, and release from darkness for the prisoners."

(Isaiah 61:1 ISV)

Daily Note

Write it & read aloud: I am anointed, because He chose me!

_____

_____

_____

_____

_____

_____

_____

_____

_____

Day 7
~Self-Love is Your Best Friend~

Writer/encourager - Nikki Banas, stated it perfectly in "Self-Love":

"Be brave enough to take off the masks you wear out there and get to know who you are underneath. Be vulnerable enough to accept your flaws and know that they are what make you human; they are what make you real. Be confident enough to accept and cherish your strengths. Don't minimize them or hide them…they are your beautiful gifts to share with the world. Be brave enough to say, you know what, all of this is who I am. I make so many mistakes. I can be forgetful, I am messy. But I am doing my best with what I've got. And

I am so proud of that. I am so proud of me. And I am proud of who I am becoming."

When all else fails – even people who fail you, you always have yourself to rely on. Be your own best friend! Take care of you. Love on you. Treat yourself kind, nurture your soul and feed yourself with positivity; your mental health is paramount. You can't rely on others to do these things for you; that's where your love for yourself comes in.

TAKE CARE OF YOU.

"For God did not give us a spirit of timidity but one of power, love, and self-discipline."

(2 Timothy 1:7 ISV)

Daily Note

What about yourself are you most PROUD of?

_____

_____

_____

_____

_____

Day 8
~Acceptance~

What makes you feel accepted? Is it someone telling you that you've done a nice job, or a pat on the back? Maybe it's a smile and a high-five. Yes - we love to be praised and accepted, but you are already accepted by our Lord and Savior. All you need to do is believe it. Kudos from man is nothing compared to the Lord's approval. It amazes me how humans get so dispirited when we aren't praised by man. It's as if our entire world is shattered when the accolades from man don't come through. Don't get discouraged! Remember with God, we are fully accepted… fully loved!

"May the words of my mouth and the meditations of my heart be acceptable in Your sight, Lord, my Rock and my Redeemer." (Psalms 19:14 ISV).

Daily Note

What makes you feel accepted?

Day 9
~Delayed, Never Denied~

As long as you live, you will go through trials and tribulations. It's inevitable. We encounter so many circumstances in our lifetime, which often leaves us wondering if what we're going through is delaying us from reaching our destiny. Be assured that when God delays something, it's because He's aware of the obstacles ahead. He's delaying the process to keep us from being hurt, not denying us of our destiny. That's what fathers do for their children - protect them from harm. God never denies us of anything concerning our purpose in life.

"The Lord is not slow about His promise, as some people understand slowness, but is being patient with you. He does not want anyone to perish, but wants everyone to repent."

(2 Peter 3:9 ISV)

Daily Note

What is delaying you from reaching your destiny?

_____

_____

_____

_____

_____

_____

_____

_____

_____

_____

_____

_____

Day 10
~Forgiveness~

Many of us have gone through so much in our lives. Things that we still cannot seem to forgive others for, not to mention that which we fail to forgive ourselves for. We suppress our feelings, suffering in silence for years: childhood trauma, teenaged drama, young adult battles, etc. One of the reasons we're unable to forgive ourselves is because we can't forgive what others have others have done to us. We've all made mistakes in our lives, bad decisions, memories that we never want to relive ever again. Rehearsing our tattered pasts can feel shameful and turn you bitter towards life. You can't live a full, healthy, happy existence hanging onto the cringeworthy parts of your past. Give it to God and let it go! You're only hurting yourself. Your health is being affected, relationships harshly impacted, unhappy because of things you cannot change. Instead of carrying that negative baggage from year to year, unpack those bags and give the pain tucked away inside them to God. Ask God for the strength to forgive those who have wronged you. Fall to your knees and ask Him to forgive you for things you've done that aren't pleasing in His sight, then truly forgive yourself and others. Stop carrying that shame around. You only get one life to live, and there is no rehearsal. Once it's over, it's over. So now is the time for you to release all that baggage, forgive and live a life of freedom!

"Be tolerant of one another and forgive each other if anyone has a complaint against another. Just as the Lord has forgiven you, you also should forgive."

(Colossians 3:13 ISV)

TAM YVONNE

Daily Note

What are you hanging onto that you need to give to God today?

_____

_____

_____

_____

_____

_____

_____

_____

_____

_____

_____

_____

_____

_____

_____

Day 11
~Stand for Something or Fall for Anything~

Alexander Hamilton - one of the Founding Fathers of the United States, once stated, "Those who stand for nothing fall for anything." Today, choose to stand for something! Don't let the world dictate your existence. As the late, great Civil Rights icon John Lewis tweeted in the summer of 2018, "Never, ever be afraid to make some noise and get in good trouble, necessary trouble."

Make a conscious effort to stand up for what is right and for yourself. Don't allow others to dictate how you are supposed to feel and how you should live the life that God gave to you. Not them…to you.

People often do their best to mentality and emotionally bash you, but you have to stand strong and stand up for your rights and your well-being, or you'll end up falling for anything told to you or spoke over you.

Live authentically! Be authentically you! You are enough, and you are wonderfully made. If you stand on nothing else, stand believing that God knew you before you were born, and He knows all the good things He created you for. Hold your head high and fall for nothing. Walk in confidence today!

"For this reason, take up the whole armor of God so that you may be able to take a stand whenever evil comes. And when you have done everything you could, you will be able to stand firm."

(Ephesians 6:13 ISV)

Daily Note

What are you standing up for today?

Day 12
~Stay Ready So You Don't Have to Get Ready~

When my publisher brought this title to me, my mind wandered back to when I first heard the actor/rapper Will Smith say, "If you stay ready, you ain't gotta get ready, and that is how I run my life." I blew it off when I first heard it, but when I think back on it now, that quote makes so much sense. In fact, it's the mindset I embraced when the coronavirus pandemic (COVID-19) of 2020 hit. It's impossible to anticipate when life is going hammer us; we must be ready for anything coming our way. Any opportunities allotted to you, seize them. Never stop learning. Every day, there's something new to learn; invest in your professional development. Always try to be intentional about your life. The awe-inspiring American poet, Dr. Maya Angelou wrote, "I've learned that people will forget what you said, people will forget what you did, but people will never forget how you made them feel." Not only in your life, but in the lives of those you encounter, be intentional about your actions and feelings. Set goals and strive hard to achieve them, whether it's something you've never done before or started but haven't had an opportunity to complete. Be intentional about it all, girl! Focus on the end and what success is going to feel and look like for YOU. Always be ready!

"You have prepared Your people Israel to be your very own people forever, and you, Lord, have become their God!"

(2 Samuel 7:24 ISV)

TAM YVONNE

Daily Note

What do you stay ready for?

Day 13
~Lord, Lead Me~

My Lord,

Today, please keep me from trying to control my own life. Father, I ask that you lead me, define me, and make me the great person You've created with purpose. Lord, please let Your light shine brightly on my life and within my soul. Be the leading force in my life today!

"I've come into the world as light, so that everyone who believes in me won't remain in the darkness."

(John 12:46 ISV)

Daily Note

Write & repeat: Lord, lead me, define me and make me who YOU want me to be.

Day 14
~Finance is King~

Ladies, whether we're single or married, we must take our finances seriously. Yes, we all want the latest Kate Spade handbag or the hottest pair of Christian Louboutin's red bottom pumps; but dropping $700 for a pair of heels or $400 for a handbag doesn't cut it…especially if you're living paycheck to paycheck. Don't be a spendthrift. Take control and stay aware of your finances. If you don't know how or where to begin - read books. If you aren't big on reading, we live in the age of technology, where anything can be learned from the comforts of home. Binge-watch videos or attend a seminar to gain perspective. Know how your money is being spent, where you're investing, and whether you have enough for an emergency fund.

Growing up, my mother taught my sister and me to set money aside for emergencies. "You never know when hard times may come," she admonished. Guess what? Those hard times came knocking at my door in 2012 when I divorced. I was forced to relocate myself and two kids under the age of eight from Charlotte, North Carolina back to Metro Atlanta, Georgia. Gratefully, I listened to my mother, and consistently set aside part of my salary towards my savings. My preparedness made the transition so much easier; I didn't have to depend on someone else's salary to relocate.

Finally, plan for your retirement. As women we tend to compromise our needs, desires and goals to make sure our children and/or spouses are secure. We must get in the habit of considering what happens when the nest becomes empty. The children may go off to college or simply move on to the adult world; Heaven forbid we lose our spouse, whether by divorce or death. Not planning for our own happiness and retirement can prove costly in the long run.

Sisters in Christ, finance is king. We should protect our finances as much as we can!

"We've also brought along some more money to buy supplies, but we don't know who put our money back into our sacks."
(Genesis 43:22 ISV)

Daily Note

Do you have financial goals? If so, what are they? If not, create some.

Day 15
~Life Lessons, The Best Teacher~

In forty years, I've learned so many lessons in life, it's impossible to document them all; however, I'll share the ones that stand out to me. I am sure many of you have learned similar lessons, too. If not, trust me - it's coming.

Lesson #1:

Becoming a mother has shown me love like I have never known. *John 15:13* states, *"No one has greater love than this, to lay down one's life for one's friends."* When you become a parent (whether by birth, adoption, fostering or caring for a niece, nephew or a grandchild), you love your child so much that you're willing to die for them. I never knew until I became a mother that I could love someone else more than I love myself; it's the best feeling in the entire world.

Lesson #2:

Love is truly all we need to make the world go around. I don't watch the news often, because I try not to feed my soul a lot of negativity. However, when I do watch, the chaos around us hurts my heart. If we'd all show more empathy and love towards one another, what a wonderful world this would be. In the Bible, you'll see that Jesus knew all that really matters is love. Love is religion, love is race, and love is belief. Love is so much more than just scripture, but scripture does tell us that *"the person who does not love does not know God, because God is love," (1 John 4:8 ISV)*. I have learned that through my thoughts, words, aspirations, and actions, that love is at the center of it all. I pray you welcome love to be the center of your world as well.

Lesson #3:

Phenomenal people must first be exceptional servants. This went over my head as a youth, but as an adult, I've come to understand exactly what serving means. See when I was younger, I'd been taught the traditional prerequisites of religion: we must serve in church, and sacrifice our time in addition to our tithes. The meaning of all this wasn't clear to me until I became stronger in my faith. I took time to look back at some of my heroes and sheroes like Dr. Martin Luther King, Jr., John Lewis, C.T. Vivian, Rosa Parks, Fannie Lou Hamer, Ida B. Wells, Mary McLeod Bethune and so many more for inspiration. These are but a few legends whom are forever immortalized, because each of them lived their lives by serving others and sticking to what they believed in. Knowing their rich history has motivated me to serve more and become the greatest me I can be. *"The greatest among you will be your servant. For those who exalt themselves will be humbled, and those who humble themselves will be exalted." (Matthew 23: 11-12 NIV).*

Lesson #4:

Whew child, how much time do you have? Because I could probably write an entire book on this topic alone. Learn how to stop worrying and live for today! I wish I could say I've mastered this, but I'm so very far from it. God knows, I literally worry about everything…because I'm constantly going to Him about it. I've gotten a lot better than I was, because I've developed a deeper relationship with the Lord. But there was a time when fear consumed me.

It started when I became a teen. I'd worry about getting good grades in school, about my parents dying, or if someone was my friend. My anxiety was on overload, but as I grew closer to God, I began releasing worry and anxiety, and learned how to live in the present and actually be present in my own life. How can you conquer worry? By trying your best every day, trusting that tomorrow will take care of itself. Live your life one day at a time, and trust God's plan for your life without worrying about if and when He's going to do it for you.

"Therefore, I tell you, do not worry about your life, what you will eat or drink; or about your body, what you will wear. Is not life more than food, and the body more than clothes? Look at the birds of the air; they do not sow or reap or store away in barns, and yet your heavenly Father feeds them. Are you not much more valuable than they? Can any one of you by worrying add a single hour to your life? Therefore, do not worry about tomorrow, for tomorrow will worry about itself. Each day has enough trouble of its own." (Matthew 6: 25-27, 34 NIV).

<u>Lesson #5:</u>

What is your passion? Each of us are given a talent by God - what is yours? Mine is writing. I discovered my passion for words at an early age, but my gift wasn't fully birthed until my debut book, *A Leap of Faith* in 2020. I knew that if I didn't use my talent, there was the possibility that I would lose it. I didn't want to lose the gift God gave me, so I sharpened my skills, released my fears and took a risk on having my work published. I didn't want to rob the world of the one thing only I can do - tell the story the way that Tam Yvonne tells it! Don't let your God-given talent rest on the surface; let that seed grow and share it with the world. Use your gift, or risk losing it. *"For to everyone who has, more will be given, and he will grow rich; but from the one who has not, even what he has will be taken away." (Matthew 25:29 NIV).*

Lesson #6:

Always be a blessing to others. I say this often. If you give to others, give genuinely and privately. Everyone doesn't need to know what you do for others. When you give genuinely, do it without expecting anything in return, whether it's praise or acknowledgement. I know from personal experience that secret giving with pure motives invites a different kind of joy to consume you. It also makes you more thankful. *"Be careful not to practice your righteous in front of others to be seen by them. If you do, you will have no reward from your Father in heaven. So, when you give to the needy, do not announce it with trumpets, as the hypocrites do in the synagogues and on the streets, to be honored by others. Truly I tell you, they have received their reward in full. But when you give to the needy, do not let your left hand know what your right hand is doing, so that your giving may be in secret. Then your Father, who sees what is done in secret, will reward you." (Matthew 6: 1-4 NIV).*

Lesson #7:

Never give up! Be persistent. Always move forward, no matter how many times you are rejected or stumble.

"Then Jesus said to them, "Suppose you have a friend, and you go to him at midnight and say, 'Friend, lend me three loaves of bread; a friend of mine on a journey has come to me, and I have no food to offer him.' And suppose the one inside answers, 'Don't bother me. The door is already locked, and my children and I are in bed. I can't get up and give you anything.' I tell you, even though he will not get up and give you the bread because of friendship, yet because of your shameless audacity[l] he will surely get up and give you as much as you need." (Luke 11: 5-8 NIV)

Lesson #8:

Always find time to connect to yourself when you aren't feeling 100%. Sometimes, you just need time alone. I've learned that it doesn't matter how much people praise, support, or love on you - if you can't uplift yourself, you're no good to you or the world.

TAM YVONNE

"After He had dismissed them, He went up on a mountainside by himself to pray. Later that night, He was there alone." (Matthew 14:23 NIV).

Lesson #9:

This lesson used to be a hard one for me, because I was always a people pleaser. That is until I wised up and realized how much people disappointed me, and how the effort I put into relationships wasn't reciprocated. That's when I decided to journey the road less travelled by myself. Not everyone is willing to go the extra mile for you, the way you would for them, whether it's a relationship or even your job. Sometimes, the best thing to do is go against your expectations and travel the road which is right for you.

"Enter through the narrow gate. For wide is the gate and broad is the road that leads to destruction, and many enter through it. But small is the gate and narrow the road that leads to life, and only a few find it." (Matthew 7: 13-14 NIV)

Lesson #10:

This lesson is considered the Golden Rule - the lesson of all lessons:

"Do to others whatever you would have them do to you." (Matthew 7:12 NIV). This applies to Christians and non-believers alike. It's really that simple - how do you want others to treat you? Do the same for and to them. You

will never go wrong in life by sticking to the Golden Rule!

What is your favorite life lesson?

_____
_____
_____
_____
_____
_____
_____
_____
_____
_____
_____
_____
_____

Day 16
~Strength~

Ladies, whether you know it or not, God delights in strong women! The Bible tells us in *Proverbs 31:25*, "*[A woman] is clothed with strength and dignity; she can laugh at the days to come.*" That verse alone makes it extremely clear that God gives women strength. It is up to us to be responsible with the strength we're given and accountable for how we use it. When you become a woman of great strength and know your purpose, it gives all glory to God and releases you from darkness and despair.

Daily Note

What is your strength?

Day 17

~ What is the Message of Job? ~

When I read the book of Job, I always think about his suffering. How his friends were ineffective in responding to him. How he struggled to understand and remain faithful. All the things that I too, have endured in my lifetime. Needing help, thinking your friends and family will come through, but no one ever shows up. Now you're struggling and have no idea how you're going to make ends meet. You don't understand how you got in this situation in the first place, and begin to question your faith, doubting God is listening to your prayers. All that Job endured; we endure in our own way.

Going through hard times doesn't make you a bad person. Bad things happen to good people, too. Job was an upright man who feared God, yet his life still unraveled. His life wasn't torn apart because he was a bad man; Job went through because of his own unwavering faithfulness to God.

Job's message also teaches us that during our struggles, we must never lose our faith in God, even in suffering. Inevitably, people will fail us. Friends, family, children, spouses...but God never does.

Always remember that the teacher (GOD) is silent during a test, but their presence is always there. No matter how difficult it gets, turn away from evil. Know that God is with you during the storm, and He is in control.

"The Lord blessed the latter days of Job more than his beginning."

(Job 42:12)

TAM YVONNE

Daily Note

What is your takeaway from the Book of Job?

Day 18
~ Keep Pressing On ~

We are 18 days into this daily journey together, and I hope you're freeing yourself from the past and pressing forward in your life. Our past experiences often hold us back from all the magnificent blessings God has in store for us. Having unresolved issues that haven't been dealt with becomes a hindrance to our progress to embrace all the goodness life has to offer. If only we could see beyond past hurts to see what gifts God has in store for us, we'd have the fire to press through our troubles and get bombarded with blessings from Heaven!

Let go of former things and embrace the new.

TAM YVONNE

"Remember ye not the former things, neither consider the things of old. Behold, I will do a new thing; now it shall spring forth; shall ye not know it? I will even make a way in the wilderness, and rivers in the desert."

Isaiah 43:18-19 (KJV)

No matter how hard it gets, ask God to help you to press towards what lies ahead for you!

Daily Note

What are you letting go of today & embracing in its place?

_____

_____

_____

_____

_____

_____

_____

_____

_____

Day 19
~ What Are You Focused On? ~

Don't let defeat, depression, anxiety, fears, bondage and sin become your focus.

Now is the time for you to shift. Focus on:
- Victory instead of defeat
- Hope instead of depression
- Love instead of fear
- Freedom instead of bondage
- Righteousness instead of sin
- Peace instead of anxiety

This is the time for you to rise and stand on God's Word, shouting His truth from the mountaintop! Set your mind on God and focus on His promise to you!

"Be strong and courageous. Don't fear or tremble before them, because the Lord your God will be the one who keeps on walking with you—He won't leave you or abandon you."
(Deuteronomy 31:6 ISV)

Daily Note

What are you shifting your focus to?

_____
_____
_____
_____
_____
_____
_____
_____
_____

Day 20
~ Where is My Boaz? ~

I purposely saved this topic for close to the end of this book, because we must first work on ourselves before we're ready for a mate, especially as a woman desiring a husband.

I can't count the number of times I've heard "Where's my Boaz," when meeting single and divorced women like myself. These are successful, wealthy, Godly women of integrity, who you'd think wouldn't have a problem finding a husband, but there's one major roadblock many of them have in common: they're working to find Boaz instead of allowing Boaz find them (the Word declares He that findeth a wife, remember?). Then, they forget to ask God to bless them with the mate He wants for them and remove negative influences from their lives.

Often, we want to control everything. Yes, I said it *(blank stare)*, because I used to be one of those ladies. I was desperate to control every single aspect of my life, right down to the man I wanted.

Well I'm here to tell you, it didn't work! I've kissed some frogs in my life, and still have no prince to show for it. Why? Because I tried to do it my way without allowing God do things His way and write my love story for me.

I insisted on holding onto the pen for myself and gripped it so tightly, eventually God had to tell me, "Okay – keep doing it your way, have at it." And I did for a long time. I was heartbroken that my stubbornness continued yielding the same results: the same type of men I thought I wanted, and not who God wanted for me.

I had to release the pen and give it back to the author of my love story. Although my tale has yet to arrive at happily ever after, I understand that it's still being written. God is preparing one of His sons specifically for me, and He'll do the same for you, if you just let go of the pen.

All we have to do is look to the book of Ruth for direction; her actions show us what to do. Ruth was a respectful woman who cared for her elders – including Naomi with her bad attitude and pity parties. Naomi was someone I don't think anyone wanted to be around during the time she was grieving her sons and husband, but sweet Ruth loved on Naomi and stuck by her, no matter how tough times got.

Ladies, we need to listen to our elders. We're living in a time when many of us have been blessed with a good education. We've obtained bachelor's degrees, masters' degrees, and doctorate degrees; all this education can cause us to believe that we know everything. No one can tell us anything, because we're "Dr. _____." In spite of the titles and degrees you've earned, always value the wisdom of your elders, whether by experience or age. Ruth could've easily disrespected her mother-in-law, but she didn't. She respected her.

The way we dress and carry ourselves is also important. When I was in college, one of my business professors taught us, "Dress for the job you want. Dress for success."

I must admit, reality television and social media have heavily influenced what society deems that we're supposed to look like. Skimpy wardrobes have become the norm; it's amazing how acceptable immodesty is now. However, in the Bible, Naomi instructed Ruth to look her best for the wealthy Boaz, who could've had any woman in the land.

Don't get me wrong – I'm not telling you what or what not to wear, but from my own personal experiences, the way you dress is a determining factor for the type of man you get. Your presentation places value on how you and others you come into contact with perceive you. Take heart ladies – your Boaz is out there waiting on you.

Daily Note

What type of man are you carrying yourself to attract?

_____

_____

_____

_____

_____

_____

_____

Day 21
~The Peace of God~

God has an open-door policy. No matter the time or the day, you can go to God, and He will be there for you. He continuously reminds us to cast our cares upon Him… He's got you. He's willing to take on our worries, hurts and concerns – all of it for us, His children!

I don't know why we have a hard time going to God. It's not like He doesn't already know what is bothering us, right? He just wants us to come to Him, so He can unburden our hearts. He wants to give us peace, even in the midst of our stressful lives. All we have to do is give our cares over to Him with thanksgiving for His love, protection, guidance and provision. Today, make a pledge to accept the peace of God in your life.

On this day, *(Day) (Month) (Year)*, I will stop dwelling on the uncertainties in my life. I will no longer worry. I cast my cares to the Lord in prayer, and welcome the peace of God to flood my heart. All my burdens I cast upon the Lord Jesus Christ. It is released!

Signed,
His Daughter (Your Name)

"Never worry about anything. Instead, in every situation let your petitions be made known to God through prayers and requests, with thanksgiving. Then God's peace, which goes far beyond anything we can imagine, will guard your hearts and minds in union with the Messiah Jesus."

(Philippians 4: 6-9 ISV)

Daily Note

TAM YVONNE

Bonus Day

"Be in awe and know that I am God. I will be exalted among the nations. I will be exalted throughout the earth."

(Psalm 46:10 ISV)

Life is our greatest blessing; however, we will experience tremendous ups and downs throughout it. We encounter all kinds of people. Some kind, some mean. No matter who we come across, only God can meet our needs. We must be still and allow Him to write our story. Be secure knowing that God created us for a purpose; all the good and bad that we encounter is all part of our story, which in turn helps build our faith, leading to a positive and promising future!

Know that man will not always be there, but God never leaves. Man will lie to you, but God's word is the truth and never changes. Man will let you down, but

TAM YVONNE

God lifts you up! Don't rely on man to fulfill your needs - depend solely on God, who meets every single one of our needs according to His riches in glory.

If you practice what I shared at the beginning of this devotional (PPF: patience, prayer and faith), there is no way you can block the blessings that God has in store for you.

"I will bless the LORD at all times; His praise will be in my mouth continuously."

(Psalm 34:1 ISV)

Epilogue

Wow! So we've already completed our days together. I hope spending time between these pages has been a time of reflection for you, as it has for me. Did you use it as an opportunity to learn to stop trying to control your own life letting God do His job of awarding you the magnificent life that He created for you? I certainly hope so.

A peaceful life is what you should strive for; you can't be at peace if you're constantly trying to manage your own life, especially without praying. Let it all go and give it to God!

It's not going to happen overnight, and requires plenty of patience, prayer and blind faith, but your breakthrough will happen. The wait will be worth it!

I hope you enjoyed this devotional as much as I enjoyed writing it. And if you haven't checked out my debut book, *A Leap of Faith,* pick up a copy for your personal library today!

Always Be a Blessing,
Tam Yvonne

Prayer

~Read it aloud & believe it! ~

Let the morning bring me word of Your unfailing love,
for I have put my trust in You.
Show me the way I should go,
for to You I entrust my life.
Rescue me from my enemies, o Lord,
for I hide myself in You.
Teach me to do Your will,
for You are my God;
may Your good spirit
lead me on level ground.
(Psalm 143:8-10 NIV)

<u>Let GOD's voice</u>
<u>be the FIRST sound you hear when you awaken.</u>

Post a copy of this verse in a location
where it will be the first thing you see in the morning.

Reflection Notes

*"Our habits will either make us or break us.
We become what we repeatedly do."*
~ Sean Covey

So it's been said that it takes 21 days to make or break a habit. We've been together for 21 days, plus a bonus day in this book, which means we've had 22 days to break those habits that have been dogging us! You should be close to finding your way to peace. I know I am.

Now is the time to STOP. To be still and reflect on what we've covered in these 22 days. Take time to focus on your spirituality, career, beliefs, family or your health.

Have you started making changes to your life? Do you plan on making changes? If so, what are they?

Write down what you want to change, and how you plan to implement those changes in your life, leading to peace.

TAM YVONNE

In this section, you can jot down your thoughts and desires. Those things you want to see changed and how you plan to get there.

Take this opportunity to discover who you are. Now it's not an overnight process - it's going to take time. Just remain PPF: patient, prayerful and faithful! BELIEVE you can, and you're halfway there!

Reflections

TAM YVONNE

BE STILL

TAM YVONNE

BE STILL

TAM YVONNE

BE STILL

TAM YVONNE

BE STILL

TAM YVONNE

TAM YVONNE

About the Author

Amazon best-selling author Tam Yvonne makes her home on the outskirts of Atlanta, Georgia with her two teenagers, *The Luv Bugs*. She has garnered acclaim for her writing, including her debut book, *A Leap of Faith*.

Tam is a lover and follower of Jesus, writer/author, motivational speaker and educator who spends most of her time reading, writing, cooking and traveling the world as she often did when growing up as an army brat.

An admitted people watcher, Tam feeds her addiction to observation by creating fictional stories and characters that are both relatable and make sense.

For updates on the goings-on of Tam Yvonne, visit www.tamtheauthor.com or follow her on these social media platforms:

 The Author Tam Yvonne

 @TamTheAuthor

www.ingramcontent.com/pod-product-compliance
Lightning Source LLC
Chambersburg PA
CBHW070940080526
44589CB00013B/1589